A Tunnel Runs Through

Runs Through

Crystal Sikkens
Crabtree Publishing Company
www.crabtreebooks.com

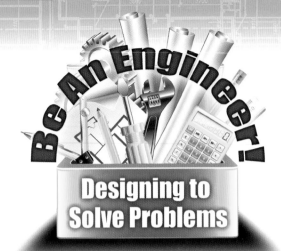

Be An Engineer! Designing to Solve Problems

Author: Crystal Sikkens

Series research and development:
Janine Deschenes and Reagan Miller

Editorial director: Kathy Middleton

Editor: Petrice Custance

Proofreader: Janine Deschenes

Design: Katherine Berti

Photo research: Crystal Sikkens

Production coordinator and prepress technician:
Tammy McGarr

Print coordinator: Margaret Amy Salter

Photographs:

Alamy: Pulsar Images p13 (top); Nick Savage p15

Getty Images: ROMEO GACAD p 16 (inset); MAURICIO LIMA p19

Shutterstock: © Kanisorn Pringthongfoo title page

Superstock: Blend Images p4

Wikimedia Commons: GeeKaa p13 (bottom)

All other images by Shutterstock

Animation and digital resources produced for
Crabtree Publishing by Plug-In Media

Library and Archives Canada Cataloguing in Publication

Sikkens, Crystal, author
          A tunnel runs through / Crystal Sikkens.

(Be an engineer! designing to solve problems)
Issued in print and electronic formats.
Includes index.
ISBN 978-0-7787-2903-7 (hardcover).--
ISBN 978-0-7787-2938-9 (softcover).--
ISBN 978-1-4271-1851-6 (HTML)

          1. Tunnels--Juvenile literature. 2. Tunnels--Design and construction--
Juvenile literature. I. Title.

TA807.S55 2017   j624.1'93   C2016-907062-X
                                                              C2016-907063-8

Library of Congress Cataloging-in-Publication Data

Names: Sikkens, Crystal, author.
Title: A tunnel runs through / Crystal Sikkens.
Description: New York, New York : Crabtree Publishing Company, [2017] |
  Series: Be an engineer! Designing to solve problems | Audience: Ages 7-10.
  | Audience: Grades 4 to 6. | Includes index.
Identifiers: LCCN 2016056400 (print) | LCCN 2016057700 (ebook) |
  ISBN 9780778729037 (reinforced library binding : alk. paper) |
  ISBN 9780778729389 (pbk. : alk. paper) |
  ISBN 9781427118516 (Electronic HTML)
Subjects: LCSH: Tunnels--Design and construction--Juvenile literature. |
  Tunnels--Juvenile literature.
Classification: LCC TA807 .S55 2017 (print) | LCC TA807 (ebook) |
  DDC 624.1--dc23
LC record available at https://lccn.loc.gov/2016056400

Crabtree Publishing Company
www.crabtreebooks.com   1-800-387-7650

Printed in Canada/032017/BF20170111

Published in Canada
Crabtree Publishing
616 Welland Ave.
St. Catharines, Ontario
L2M 5V6

Published in the United States
Crabtree Publishing
PMB 59051
350 Fifth Avenue, 59th Floor
New York, New York 10118

Published in the United Kingdom
Crabtree Publishing
Maritime House
Basin Road North, Hove
BN41 1WR

Published in Australia
Crabtree Publishing
3 Charles Street
Coburg North
VIC 3058

Contents

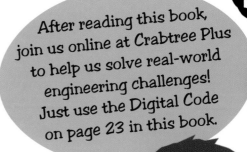

Hi, I'm Ava and this is Finn. Get ready for an inside look at the world of engineering! The Be an Engineer! series explores how engineers build structures to solve problems.

After reading this book, join us online at Crabtree Plus to help us solve real-world engineering challenges! Just use the Digital Code on page 23 in this book.

Crossing the River

Every morning Tyler's mom drives him to school. His school is on the other side of a river that runs through the city. One morning, the bridge they use to cross the river was closed because it was damaged by high winds. This seemed to happen often. On their way back home, Tyler wondered if there was a better way to cross the river.

Another Way Across

Tyler thought about using a boat to get across the river, but if the weather was bad, a boat might not be safe. Then he thought of a tunnel. A tunnel could go under the river, and could be used in both good and bad weather. Tyler thought a tunnel would be the perfect solution.

> *A tunnel is a tube-shaped passageway built under ground or water, or through a mountain.*

Did you know?

Subways are tunnels built under busy cities. They use **electric** railroads to move people from one place to another.

3.5m

What Is an Engineer?

Are you like Tyler and enjoy finding solutions to problems? If so, maybe one day you'll use your problem-solving skills in a career as an engineer! An engineer is a person who uses math, science, and creative thinking to design things that solve problems and meet needs.

Some engineers design buildings and structures that solve problems or meet needs, such as bridges, skyscrapers, and tunnels.

Different Kinds

There are many different kinds of engineers. You could be an engineer that works on equipment that goes into space, or one that finds ways to protect the environment. You could even be an engineer that designs things that improve health care and medicine!

Steps to Solving Problems

All engineers follow a set of steps that help them find a solution to the problem they need to solve. This set of steps is known as the Engineering Design Process. Engineers may repeat the steps as many times as necessary in order to make sure their solution is both safe and **effective**.

The Engineering Design Process

1 ASK
Ask questions and gather information about the problem you are trying to solve.

2 BRAINSTORM
Work with a group to come up with different ideas to solve the problem. Choose the best solution.

3 PLAN AND MAKE A MODEL
Create a plan to carry out your solution. Draw a diagram and gather materials. Make a **model** of your solution.

4 TEST AND IMPROVE
Test your model and record the results. Using the results, improve, or make your design better. Retest your improved design.

5 COMMUNICATE
Share your design with others.

Asking Questions

The Engineering Design Process begins with engineers asking questions and gathering information about a problem. If an engineer is trying to find the best way for people to cross a river, they might look at what the normal weather conditions are for the area, or how many people need to get across.

An engineer might also do research to find out what the land is like around and below the river.

Brainstorming

Once an engineer has done their research, gathered information, and found answers to their questions, they brainstorm, or discuss with others, ways they can solve the problem.

When brainstorming, engineers might use diagrams such as this to help them organize ideas.

Use boats to move people across the river

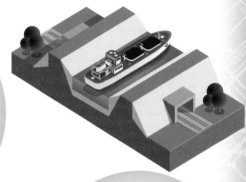

Fly people over the river in airplanes

Problem

High winds often damage the only bridge over a river

Tear down the bridge and build a tunnel under the river

Build another bridge to use when the main one gets damaged

Tear down the bridge, fill in the river, and create roads over top

Creating a Plan

After brainstorming, the group decides on the best idea. If they decide a tunnel is the best option, the engineer must spend a lot of time planning how to build the tunnel. How a tunnel is built depends a lot on the type of rock and soil it will be going through. Most tunnels can be divided into three or four main types.

Did you know?

Many animals, such as chipmunks, also build tunnels. Some animals dig small tunnels to hide or stay cool. Other animals build homes with many connected tunnels.

*Soft ground and soft rock tunnels are built into mud, sand, or soft rock, such as limestone and shale. Special machines known as **tunnel boring machines (TBM)** are often used to drill the tunnels. They give extra support during construction until an iron or **concrete** lining is installed.*

*(left) Many hard rock tunnels are built using TBMs or **explosives** that blast through hard rock, such as granite. Extra support and lining for these tunnels may not be necessary.*

*Underwater tunnels are often started by digging a **trench** in the bottom of a lake, river, or ocean. Pre-made steel or concrete tubes (shown above) are lowered into the trench, joined, and covered with rocks. The water is then pumped out of the tunnel.*

Making a Model

Once an engineer has determined the type of tunnel to be built, he or she will create a model of it. A model is a **representation** of a real object. It is a smaller version of the real thing. An engineer may use a model to explain their design to the team building the tunnel.

A model can be designed on a computer or tablet, or be a **3-D** object.

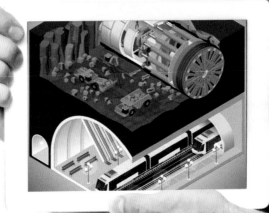

Testing the Tunnel

Engineers also use their model to test the design of the tunnel. The model helps them learn if the tunnel is strong enough to support the surrounding rock, and whether the tunnel will disturb the **environment** that is above it.

An engineer may do many tests with their model. After each test, the engineer records the results and makes any necessary improvements.

Sharing the Results

After an engineer has finished testing and improving the design of their tunnel, they share their results with others. Sharing their results helps future engineers design stronger tunnels using less dangerous methods of drilling, and creating less impact on the environment.

Using Past Information

Sharing results also helps engineers learn which designs and methods worked and which ones did not. They can also better determine what the best size of tunnel would be, depending on the tunnel's purpose, and what shape is the most **stable**.

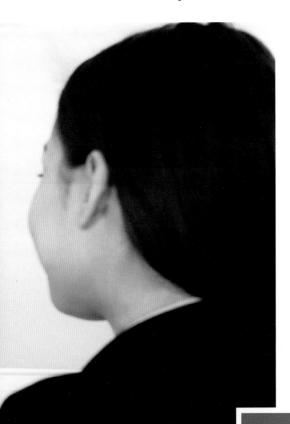

Did you know?

Tunnels are not only built for transportation. They are also used for **mining**, and to move water or **sewage**.

By sharing information, tunnels around the world can be built using safer machines, such as tunnel boring machines.

Important Steps

Building a tunnel is a dangerous job. If it is not done correctly, a tunnel can collapse, or cave in, putting people's lives in danger and causing damage to the surrounding land. The Engineering Design Process is an important tool that helps to make sure engineers design safe and strong tunnels.

Tunnel Collapse

On January 12, 2007, a subway station tunnel collapsed in São Paulo, Brazil. One of the main causes of the collapse was poor planning and design. It is believed the rock above the tunnel was heavier than the engineer planned for. The lining and supports could not hold the weight of the heavy rocks. This caused the tunnel roof to first crack, and then collapse.

Seven people lost their lives when the São Paulo tunnel collapsed.

Try it Out!

If the engineer working on the São Paulo subway tunnel had used a model to test heavy rock types, this disaster may have been avoided. Try this yourself by building a tunnel and testing its strength.

You will need:

modeling clay or Play-doh

a popsicle stick or a pencil

Five books of different weights

pitcher of water

Instructions:

1. Create a log out of your clay that is about 6 inches (15 cm) long and about 5 inches (12.7 cm) high.

2. Use your popsicle stick or pencil to carve out a horizontal tunnel at least 1.5 inches (3.8 cm) wide by 2.5 inches (6.4 cm) high. The tunnel must go from one end of the clay log to the other.

3. Slowly pour water over the clay. Look for cracks that are allowing water to leak into your tunnel. If you found leaks, how could you repair them?

4. Next, place the lightest book on your clay tunnel.
   - Continue placing the other four books, lightest to heaviest, on top.
   - Was your tunnel able to hold all five books? If your tunnel collapsed, how could you improve your model to make it stronger?

Avoiding Disaster

Following all the steps in the Engineering Design Process can sometimes take years to complete. Taking the time to closely follow each step is always important, because people's safety and lives depend on engineers designing safe, strong, and long-lasting tunnels.

The Laerdal Tunnel in Norway is the world's longest road tunnel. The tunnel has special features such as colored lights to help keep tired drivers alert, and to comfort people who don't like being in small spaces.

Learning More

Books

Mattern, Joanne. *Tunnels* (Engineering Wonders). Rourke Educational Media, 2015.

Pettiford, Rebecca. *Tunnels* (Amazing Structures). Jump!, 2015.

Loh-Hagan, Virginia. *Tunnels* (21st Century Junior Library: Extraordinary Engineering). Cherry Lake Publishing, 2017.

Websites

Take the Tunnel Challenge and pick the correct tool for digging a tunnel in different types of ground at: **www.pbs.org/wgbh/buildingbig/ tunnel/challenge/index.html**

Find out more about different tunnel types and uses at: **http://easyscienceforkids.com/ all-about-tunnels/**

For fun engineering challenges, activities, and more, enter the code at the Crabtree Plus website below.

www.crabtreeplus.com/be-an-engineer

Your code is:
bae04

Glossary

Note: Some boldfaced words are defined where they appear in the book.

3-D (THREE-DEE) *adjective* Short for three-dimensional, an object that has length, width, and height

concrete (KON-kreet) *noun* A hard, strong building material

effective (ih-FEK-tiv) *adjective* Producing the correct result

electric (ih-LEK-trik) *adjective* Produced or operated by electricity, a type of energy

environment (en-VAHY-ern-muh-nt) *noun* The natural surroundings of things

explosive (ik-SPLOH-siv) *noun* A device that explodes, or blows up

mining (MAHY-ning) *noun* The process of digging for minerals, such as coal or diamonds, in the ground

model (MOD-l) *noun* A representation of a real object

representation *noun* (rep-ri-zen-TEY-shun) Something that stands in place for something else

sewage (SOO-ij) *noun* Waste from sinks, toilets, showers, and other devices in a home or building

stable (STEY-buh-l) *adjective* Does not change position

trench (trench) *noun* A ditch that is long and narrow

tunnel boring machine (TBM) (TUHN-l BOHR-ing muh-SHEEN) *noun* A machine used to dig circular tunnels through soil or rock; also known as a "mole"

A noun is a person, place, or thing. An adjective is a word that tells you what something is like.

Index